Seeking Answers, Finding Rest

Through Prayer

Hart Ramsey

Sermon To Book
www.sermontobook.com

Seeking Answers, Finding Rest / Hart Ramsey
ISBN-13: 978-1-945793-11-0
ISBN-10: 1-945793-11-2

This book is dedicated to the intercessors in churches around the world who spend many a waking moment standing, kneeling, laying, and crying before God on behalf of those who need Him so desperately. On behalf of all of us.

May we all sense the call to join this faithful remnant of prayer warriors who believe not only in prayer, but above all in the God of their prayers.

CONTENTS

Unanswered Prayer

According to *The Complete Word Study Dictionary*, the Greek word for praying is *proseuchomai*.[1] This is made up of the prefix *pros* and the root *euchomai*.

The verb *euchomai* originally meant "to speak your desire; to say what you want; to articulate what's in your heart." The prefix *pros* is a directional prefix that means either 'to' or 'towards.' When you put the two parts together, you have this definition for prayer: "to verbalize your desires to God."

Do you verbalize your desires to God? Do you say what's in your heart?

We tend to start feeling prayerful when life is less than perfect. When we are dissatisfied or in trouble, we ask God for anything we think will help: blessings, guidance, revenge, deliverance. Maybe when we do this, everything works out right away. No one has a problem with God when prayer is a matter of instant gratification, but that isn't always the case.

When we pray and God doesn't give us what we ask for, we become offended, discouraged, and doubtful. We nurse grudges against God because we think our prayers went unheard. Our indictment is either against God for not keeping His end of the bargain or against ourselves for not being spiritual enough to get a prayer answered. We start to question God's goodness and His ability, perhaps even His existence.

If He is so powerful and so good, why did He let these things happen? Why didn't He prevent this? Why didn't He give me what I needed? Is He even there?

Chances are, whether you've been a Christian for twenty years or twenty days, you've had times when you prayed and it seemed no answer was forthcoming. When this happens, don't shake your fist at heaven or figure God has better things to do with His time than pay attention to your problems. Don't assume He has given up on you or labeled you a lost cause. The issue is not with God but with your misunderstanding and mishandling of prayer. You have some perspectives that are keeping you from experiencing an effective prayer life.

This book will show you what you need to know about getting your prayers answered. The real question is: Are you ready to hear it?

CHAPTER 1

Covenant Confusion

The prayer life of the twenty-first-century Christian is in danger of death by cliché.

Our idea of prayer has become trapped in a set of overly familiar sayings that roll off the tongue so easily we don't give them a second thought.

How many times have we said, "I'll be praying for you" or "I'm sending prayers your way," only to forget to follow up with actual prayer? Then there's the questionably reassuring "My thoughts and prayers are with you," which is just a vaguely religious way of saying, "I see you're going through a tough time. I feel bad for you." When we really want something, we may go with "I'm hoping and praying," which makes prayer sound like a wish-upon-a-star roll of the dice.

Corporately, we may find ourselves called upon to take part in a "moment of silence." This is the kind of language you'd expect to find in secular settings, and it has no place in the church. Why would we opt for thinking quietly about the issue at hand when we could be bringing it before the throne of God?

Our understanding of prayer is tied up in these appropriately solemn sayings that look good on a bumper sticker or a get-well card but cut prayer off at the knees and tear out its heart. We may be ready to say without hesitation that prayer changes things, but are we truly engaging in life-transforming, radically humbling, soul-satisfying conversation with the Most High God?

While some prayer clichés gloss over the true power of prayer and distract us from unleashing it, others contribute to confusion about how we should pray.

Take, for example, "Let's touch and agree." Matthew 18:19 of the King James Bible reads, *"Again I say unto you, That if two of you shall agree on earth as touching any thing that they shall ask, it shall be done for them of my Father which is in heaven."* We read this verse and think we need to touch in order for our prayers to be answered, but that's not the case. The word 'touching' here is a translation of a Greek word that means 'concerning.'[2]

In 1 Corinthians 8:1, Paul wrote, *"Now as touching things offered unto idols, we know that we all have knowledge. Knowledge puffeth up, but charity edifieth"* (KJV). There it is again: 'touching.' However, the New Living Translation reads, *"Now regarding your question about food that has been offered to idols"* (1 Corinthians 8:1 NLT). The word 'touching' in this context doesn't mean putting your hand on it; again, it means concerning it or regarding it.

If we refer to Matthew 18:19 in the New Living Translation, we find that there shouldn't be a doctrine of touching and agreeing, just agreeing: *"I also tell you this: If two of you agree here on earth concerning anything you ask, my Father in heaven will do it for you"* (NLT). We don't need to touch and agree; we need to agree. Touching won't help if we're not agreeing, and touching won't make us agree. It's a heart issue.

We've also gone off track with our understanding of the special ending we're instructed to tack on each prayer: "in the name of Jesus" or "in Jesus' name." We can fall into the habit of treating it like the "abracadabra" of the prayer formula, the wave of the magic wand that will cause everything we desire to materialize. Well, if it isn't the key phrase that sets the magic in motion, why do we bother saying it?

'In Jesus' name' is a power of attorney phrase. We are saying to God that we come to Him as submitted representatives of Christ and we feel confident in our prayer because of Jesus' promises. Jesus told His disciples, *"I appointed you to go and produce lasting fruit, so that the Father will give you whatever you ask for, using my name"* (John 15:16 NLT). When we finish our prayers with "in Jesus' name," we are saying, "Jesus sent me."

So far we've focused on the mild, everyday prayer clichés—the ones we use on a regular basis when we're not too worked up—but what about the ones we whip out on special occasions? We reserve a supply of rallying battle cries for when we want to drive up the intensity in the room. When we're ready to see the power of God loosed right here and now in this very place, we'll boldly declare, "We're going to storm the gates of heaven!" or "We're about to press through the veil!" Excitement rises. Hearts are racing. Blood is pumping. The volume goes up. "Surely this should get us the results we desire!"

It's easy to believe that louder praying will get better results. After all, if we're catapulting our voices to heaven and beating down God's door, He is more likely to get the message, right? Wrong.

When Jesus was instructing His disciples how and how not to pray, He told them:

> *When you pray, don't be like the hypocrites who love to pray publicly on street corners and in the synagogues where everyone can see them. I tell you the truth, that is all the reward they will ever get. But when you pray, go away by yourself, shut the door behind you, and pray to your Father in private. Then your Father, who sees everything, will reward you.*
>
> *When you pray, don't babble on and on as the Gentiles do. They think their prayers are answered merely by repeating their words again and again. Don't be like them, for your Father knows exactly what you need even before you ask him!* **— Matthew 6:5–8 (NLT)**

This is not to say that we should never pray with other Christians but always alone. It means the outward expression of our prayer is not what makes the difference. God sees the private things. He sees what's in our hearts and on our minds. We don't have to yell to get

His attention or say the same thing over and over to make it stick. God already knows.

Louder praying may feel more expressive or exciting, but never mistake volume for anointing.

The King James Version of James 5:16 reads, *"The effectual fervent prayer of a righteous man availeth much"* (KJV). Fervent praying may sometimes get louder as it goes along, but it's not the outer volume that gets results; it's the inner passion. What counts is the sincerity of heart. When we care deeply about something and we earnestly ask for God's help, we don't have to ask loudly. He hears us.

These two prayer clichés in particular—"We're going to press through the veil" and "We're about to storm the gates of heaven"— have a bigger problem than volume. They're theologically flawed. They belong to a school of thought concerning prayer that's based on Old Covenant beliefs. The truth is that we don't need to press through the veil and we certainly don't need to storm the gates of heaven. To understand why, we'll have to clear up the covenant confusion.

"A Far Better Covenant"

In the Old Testament, we read of the many rules and regulations God put in place so inherently imperfect people could worship Him, the perfect God. He gave them specific instructions for the who, what, when, where, and why of approaching Him. He set up a system of animal sacrifice and various offerings and gifts for the atonement (forgiving) of sin and fellowship with Him.

He established a priesthood led by a high priest, who was the main figure between God and the people. God also selected a specific location where they would worship Him and His presence would be with them there (Deuteronomy 12; 2 Chronicles 7).

The problem with this system was that people could never get it right. They were always messing up and falling short of the goal. God knew this would be the case. He had a plan for a new covenant:

> *The law of Moses was unable to save us because of the weakness of our sinful nature. So God did what the law could not do. He sent his own Son in a body like the bodies we sinners have. And in that body God declared an end to sin's control over us by giving his Son as a sacrifice for our sins. He did this so that the just requirement of the law would be fully satisfied for us, who no longer follow our sinful nature but instead follow the Spirit.* — **Romans 8:3–4 (NLT)**

The new system that allows people to have a relationship with God is not based on human performance. It's based on work that God has already accomplished in the death and resurrection of His Son. Jesus said, *"I am the way, the truth, and the life. No one can come to the Father except through me"* (John 14:6 NLT). Entering the presence of God is not something human beings could achieve by our own effort. We needed Christ to do the work we could not do and make a way for us to be with God.

This New Covenant is *"a far better covenant with God, based on better promises"* (Hebrews 8:6 NLT).

Jesus Himself is the High Priest, and He mediates the relationship between believers and God eternally (Hebrews 7:23–25, 28). The sacrifice Jesus offered for the atonement of human sin was His own blood, and it was the one perfect sacrifice that could satisfy the requirements of the law once and for all—for everyone who believes in Jesus Christ as the Son of God and accepts Him as the only Savior (Romans 8:3–4; Hebrews 7:25–28, 8:3, 9:12–15, 10:1–18).

All we need to draw close to God under the New Covenant is faith. Our salvation is not based on our own strength or ability. We need simply to buy into the new system God has put in place and receive the promise of an eternal life of fellowship with Him.

The temple is no longer a building in a specified location but rather the body of every believer, which now houses the Holy Spirit (1 Corinthians 6:19). Our High Priest doesn't serve on earth but at the right hand of God the Father in heaven (Hebrews 8:1–2, 9:11; Romans 8:34). Through Christ every believer has access to God, and God can develop a personal relationship with each of us. Many of us pray from an Old Covenant mentality of distance between God and us when what we have now is a direct line of communication:

> *And so, dear brothers and sisters, we can boldly enter heaven's Most Holy Place because of the blood of Jesus. By his death, Jesus opened a new and life-giving way through the curtain into the Most Holy Place. And since we have a great High Priest who rules over God's house, let us go right into the presence of God with sincere hearts fully trusting him. For our guilty consciences*

have been sprinkled with Christ's blood to make us clean, and our bodies have been washed with pure water. — Hebrews 10:19–22 (NLT)

We pray like we need to fight our way into the presence of God, storming the gates of heaven and pressing through the veil; but the gates have been opened for us and the veil torn by our Savior, Jesus Christ. We have the Spirit of the Holy God in us, and we have been marked for eternal life. Heaven isn't closed to us anymore; it's now our home.

CHAPTER 2

Know Where You Stand

To illustrate the point further, Jesus told them this story: "A man had two sons. The younger son told his father, 'I want my share of your estate now before you die.' So his father agreed to divide his wealth between his sons.

"A few days later this younger son packed all his belongings and moved to a distant land, and there he wasted all his money in wild living. About the time his money ran out, a great famine swept over the land, and he began to starve. He persuaded a local farmer to hire him, and the man sent him into his fields to feed the pigs. The young man became so hungry that even the pods he was feeding the pigs looked good to him. But no one gave him anything.

"When he finally came to his senses, he said to himself, 'At home even the hired servants have food enough to spare, and here I am dying of hunger! I will go home to my father and say, "Father, I have sinned against both heaven and you, and I am no longer worthy of being called your son. Please take me on as a hired servant."'

"So he returned home to his father. And while he was still a long way off, his father saw him coming. Filled with love and compassion, he ran to his son, embraced

*him, and kissed him. His son said to him, 'Father, I have
sinned against both heaven and you, and I am no longer
worthy of being called your son.'*

*"But his father said to the servants, 'Quick! Bring the
finest robe in the house and put it on him. Get a ring for
his finger and sandals for his feet. And kill the calf we
have been fattening. We must celebrate with a feast, for
this son of mine was dead and has now returned to life.
He was lost, but now he is found.' So the party began."*
— *Luke 15:11–24 (NLT)*

How many times do we avoid prayer because we feel
the weight of our guilt? We figure God could never want
people like us. We've done too much wrong in our lives.
We're too far gone. We really messed things up this
time, and there's no way God would want anything to do
with us. If we were to go before God and try to start a
conversation, He would probably just lose it and say:
"How dare you show your face around here after what
you've done!"

Jesus painted a different picture. He described a father
who threw all decorum to the wind and raced out to meet
his son who had squandered his money and pursued a
life of sin. This father didn't reject his son. He didn't
say, "You made your bed; now lie in it. Turn around and
go back where you came from. You're not wanted here!"
Instead, he gave his son an accepting hug and threw a
party to celebrate his return.

Sometimes we think we aren't allowed to pray
because we are being punished for our sins, but
refraining from prayer is a punishment we are inflicting
on ourselves. We think if we can get our performance up

to snuff, then we can go to Him. This is not the system God has put in place for believers in Christ.

A Solid Standing

When we read that the *"earnest prayer of a righteous person has great power and produces wonderful results"* (James 5:16 NLT), we may take it to mean that God only answers the prayers of perfect people. This is a misunderstanding of the concept of righteousness, which is a reference not to our performance but to our standing before God—or where we stand with God.

Paul's letter to the Romans sheds some light on this issue of right standing with God:

> *We are made right with God by placing our faith in Jesus Christ. And this is true for everyone who believes, no matter who we are.* — **Romans 3:22 (NLT)**

> *... God will also count us as righteous if we believe in him, the one who raised Jesus our Lord from the dead. He was handed over to die because of our sins, and he was raised to life to make us right with God.* — **Romans 4:24–25 (NLT)**

> *Therefore, since we have been made right in God's sight by faith, we have peace with God because of what Jesus Christ our Lord has done for us.* — **Romans 5:1 (NLT)**

And since we have been made right in God's sight by the blood of Christ, he will certainly save us from God's condemnation. — **Romans 5:9 (NLT)**

So now there is no condemnation for those who belong to Christ Jesus. And because you belong to him, the power of the life-giving Spirit has freed you from the power of sin that leads to death. — **Romans 8:1–2 (NLT)**

Believers in Christ stand in a position of righteousness before God, not because of our own actions but because of Christ's sacrificial death, which atoned for the sins of all who accept Him as God's Son and our Savior. We don't have to worry that God will condemn us if we go to Him. We are at peace with God. He accepts us if we believe in His Son. It's a done deal.

We don't have to worry that we aren't good enough to have a relationship with God because where we stand with God isn't based on us. It's based on who God is and what He has done, is doing, and will do. He isn't going to take one look at our messy lives and bad choices and say, "I've changed my mind. This isn't going to work. This one is a lost cause." God will never back out or fall through. He is completely reliable: *"He never changes or casts a shifting shadow"* (James 1:17 NLT). Scripture tells us that *"Jesus Christ is the same yesterday, today, and forever"* (Hebrews 13:8 NLT). God has done the work and put everything in place. All we need to do is go to Him.

When God reconciled humankind to Him through the death and resurrection of Jesus, He didn't arrange for us a position as slaves. He made us His friends:

*For since our **friendship** with God was restored by the death of his Son while we were still his enemies, we will certainly be saved through the life of his Son. So now we can rejoice in our wonderful new relationship with God because our Lord Jesus Christ has made us friends of God. — Romans 5:10–11 (NLT, emphasis added)*

We are not only God's friends but also His family:

*For all who are led by the Spirit of God are **children** of God.*

*So you have not received a spirit that makes you fearful slaves. Instead, you received God's Spirit when he adopted you as his own **children**. Now we call him, "Abba, Father." For his Spirit joins with our spirit to affirm that we are God's children. And since we are his children, we are his heirs. In fact, together with Christ we are heirs of God's glory....*

*For God knew his people in advance, and he chose them to become like his Son, so that his Son would be the firstborn among many **brothers and sisters**. And having chosen them, he called them to come to him. And having called them, he gave them right standing with himself. And having given them right standing, he gave them his glory. — Romans 8:14–17, 29–30 (NLT, emphasis added)*

Believers enjoy a position as children of God. He handpicked us to be part of His family, heirs of eternal life. God loves us. He has proven it. He went to great lengths, doing what no one else could do, to make us His children, and He has placed the Holy Spirit inside of us. He is our Father and our God, and He will help us when we pray to Him.

We must pray from our position in Jesus—our right standing. We must believe that the finished work of Christ makes us God's children and friends. Without this, we will never understand the truth of why we can and should expect good things from God:

> If God is for us, who can ever be against us? Since he did not spare even his own Son but gave him up for us all, won't he also give us everything else? — **Romans 8:31–32 (NLT)**

> "You parents—if your children ask for a loaf of bread, do you give them a stone instead? Or if they ask for a fish, do you give them a snake? Of course not! So if you sinful people know how to give good gifts to your children, how much more will your heavenly Father give good gifts to those who ask him." — **Matthew 7:9–11 (NLT)**

If God loves us so much and wants to give us good things, why do we still have trouble in this world? Does our suffering mean that God has taken away His love? Paul assured us that this is not the case:

> Can anything ever separate us from Christ's love? Does it mean he no longer loves us if we have trouble or calamity, or are persecuted, or hungry, or destitute, or in danger, or threatened with death? (As the Scriptures say, "For your sake we are killed every day; we are being slaughtered like sheep.") No, despite all these things, overwhelming victory is ours through Christ, who loved us. — **Romans 8:35–37 (NLT)**

How can we have victory when it seems like trouble is closing in from every direction? Let's remember that Christ also had trouble. He suffered a great deal. Paul wrote, *"But if we are to share his glory, we must also share his suffering. Yet what we suffer now is nothing compared to the glory he will reveal to us later"* (Romans 8:17–18 NLT).

Whether our lives in this world are easy or hard is not an indication of whether God loves us and has forgiven us. God has given us a bigger picture, an eternal perspective. No matter how bad things get down here, we have the enduring hope of everlasting life with God and a future with no suffering at all.

Even while we are still on earth, we can trust *"that God causes everything to work together for the good of those who love God and are called according to his purpose for them"* (Romans 8:28 NLT). This includes difficulties. Scripture encourages us not to consider hardship a bad thing:

> *Dear brothers and sisters, when troubles of any kind come your way, consider it an opportunity for great joy. For you know that when your faith is tested, your endurance has a chance to grow. So let it grow, for when your endurance is fully developed, you will be perfect and complete, needing nothing.* **— James 1:2–4 (NLT)**

> *We can rejoice, too, when we run into problems and trials, for we know that they help us develop endurance. And endurance develops strength of character, and character strengthens our confident hope of salvation.* **— Romans 5:3–4 (NLT)**

When we are going through hard times, we may be tempted to think that God doesn't care about us or that He is trying to punish us. The distance we put between us and God during those times only makes things worse. He doesn't want the distance. We are the ones erecting walls when we should be looking for how we can grow in our relationship with God through all circumstances of life. This is an important part of our development program.

God isn't out to get us. He isn't looking to make us pay for all that we did against Him. God is *"not willing that any should perish, but that all should come to repentance"* (2 Peter 3:9 KJV). In fact, *"there is joy in the presence of God's angels when even one sinner repents"* (Luke 15:10 NLT).

It's important that we learn to trust in God and the truth of His Word regardless of how we feel. Our right standing has already been established. It has nothing to do with our ability to perform. It has nothing to do with our rap sheet or our résumé. It has nothing to do with our pedigree, our recent failure, our pending court case, the judge's verdict, or the doctor's report.

God did the work Himself. He dealt with our sin through the blood of Jesus Christ. We have been washed clean. We must have faith in what God says He has done, even if it doesn't make sense to us, *"for God can be trusted to keep his promise"* (Hebrews 10:23 NLT).

Approaching God

When we pray, we don't have to fear rejection. We can approach God boldly because of our faith in His promises and in the work of Christ. We can't call on Him from a position of self-righteousness—as people who have done good things, followed the rules, and avoided getting into trouble, or at least are better than those other guys over there, whose lives are a total wreck—and expect Him to answer our prayers. Anything we could bring to the table would never be enough. We must come to Him as the people Jesus died to save. It's only because God's Spirit is in us and Jesus' blood covers us that we enjoy a favorable relationship with God.

Scripture tells us that we are God's *"prized possession"* (James 1:18 NLT), but we shouldn't let it go to our heads. We can be confident in our prayers, but we should never be demanding: *"Because of our faith, Christ has brought us into this place of undeserved privilege where we now stand, and we confidently and joyfully look forward to sharing God's glory"* (Romans 5:2 NLT). Our right standing with God is always undeserved because *"everyone has sinned; we all fall short of God's glorious standard"* (Romans 3:23 NLT). We must always approach God with humble gratitude, fully aware of the discrepancy between what we deserve and what God gives us.

When God answers our prayers, it isn't payment for something we did right. We should thank God every moment of every day that He doesn't give us the payment we deserve! *"For the wages of sin is death, but the free gift of God is eternal life through Christ Jesus our Lord"* (Romans 6:23 NLT). No matter how much good we do in our lives, without Jesus covering our sins, we deserve death. But instead, God gives us life.

If Jesus' sacrifice atoned for our sins, does it not matter anymore if we sin? Let's take another look at the parable of the prodigal son. The son who had gone astray was on his way back when his father ran out to greet him. He had turned back towards home. He repented and confessed his sin. His father didn't go to him when he was living sinfully; he embraced him with joy when he returned.

If we are deliberately living in sin and rebelling against God, going our own way and refusing to do what He tells us is right, we can't expect Him to be okay with that. God is always disappointed when we live beneath our intended potential. He will come out to meet us and extend grace to us, but only if we are choosing to turn to Him. He gives us the freedom to choose. The ball is always in our court.

Sin doesn't end after the moment of salvation when we initially receive Christ. We don't instantly become perfect. We still have to contend with the sinful nature until our current bodies die. What happens when we sin after we're saved? Is it all over? Have we lost our chance? Do we have to face God's judgment?

We find our answer to this concern in 1 John 1:8–9: *"If we claim we have no sin, we are only fooling ourselves and not living in the truth. But if we confess our sins to him, he is faithful and just to forgive us our sins and to cleanse us from all wickedness"* (NLT). If we honestly confess our sins to God and ask for forgiveness, He has promised to grant it to us and purify us.

Some Christians believe repentance is a one-and-done item off the checklist, but that's not how Jesus put it. Jesus taught us to pray, *"Give us this day our daily bread. And forgive us our debts"* (Matthew 6:11–12 KJV). Confession is not a one-time thing when we accept Jesus as Savior. This is a daily prayer. We need to seek God's forgiveness every day because we are going to fall short every day. We need to choose to turn back to God every time, or our sin will be allowed to build and start to take over our lives.

When we do something that displeases God, we should neither dismiss it as insignificant nor avoid Him for fear of punishment. We need to go straight to God and confess. If we do this, He has promised to forgive us because of the atoning work Jesus Christ already accomplished. He doesn't want us to put the brakes on our relationship with Him until we have everything right. He wants us to come to Him as we are and accept the position of a child, an heir, and a friend that only He could make possible.

We shouldn't become discouraged, thinking we are fighting a losing battle because we keep messing up even though we know how God wants us to live. We are fighting a battle that has already been won. The end is already decided for those who choose the salvation God offers in Christ over a life ruled by our sinful nature: *"But those who live to please the Spirit will harvest everlasting life from the Spirit. So let's not get tired of doing what is good. At just the right time we will reap a harvest of blessing if we don't give up"* (Galatians 6:8–9 NLT). In the future, our bodies will *"be released from sin and suffering"* (Romans 8:23 NLT). We have the ultimate hope to hold on to when we feel like failures. God has already made our future with Him secure.

Forgiving Others

There is something that will keep God from forgiving our sins and will block our prayers, maybe without our even realizing it. Jesus told us to pray that God would *"forgive us our sins, as we have forgiven those who sin against us"* (Matthew 6:12 NLT). He followed up on this point to make sure we didn't miss it: *"If you forgive those who sin against you, your heavenly Father will forgive you. But if you refuse to forgive others, your Father will not forgive your sins"* (Matthew 6:14–15 NLT). At another time, He said, *"But when you are praying, first forgive anyone you are holding a grudge against, so that your Father in heaven will forgive your sins, too"* (Mark 11:25 NLT).

Forgiving others stems from being forgiven, and forgiving others is a prerequisite for receiving God's forgiveness for our own sins. It's an indispensable part of our prayer, as much as God forgiving us. If we want to be forgiven, we have to forgive.

This is something that God takes very seriously. Jesus told a parable about a servant whose master forgave his extensive debt (Matthew 18:23–35). The servant then turned around and refused to forgive the debt of one of his fellow servants. The story did not end well for the unforgiving servant. His master withdrew his mercy and inflicted on the servant the punishment he was due. We do not want that to happen to us. So it is necessary for us to forgive early and forgive often.

Here's the hardest part: Jesus didn't specify the degree of offense or distinguish between different types. He instructed us to forgive each and every wrong committed against us, no matter how bad it was or how much it still hurts. That doesn't seem fair, does it? But then again, His grace covers all of our sins, regardless of how many or how terrible they are. Look at it like this: the death of Christ paid for all of the sins you have ever committed and all of the sins that have been ever committed against you. Seeing it in this light makes forgiving others more understandable.

Forgiving others is an extension of the grace we have been given. It isn't about the other person so much as it's about our own hearts. It shows we understand that we need forgiveness and don't deserve it. It also positions us to reflect God's nature to a world in desperate need of grace and reconciliation.

The restoration of relationships is important to God. If we're tempted to think it wasn't as difficult for Him, we need to think again. Remember what God went through to reconcile us to Him. Think of how Christ suffered. Consider how God had to sacrifice His own Son to make a way for us to be with Him.

Is there really any grudge we hold so dear that we are willing to sacrifice our relationship with God and reject

His blessings? Would we really choose a grievance over eternal life or a grudge over God Himself?

As God's dearly loved children, let's be mindful to allow His grace to flow through us and define our relationships with Him and everyone else. Only then will our prayers be answered.

CHAPTER 3

Getting Answers

Then Jesus went with them to the olive grove called Gethsemane, and he said, "Sit here while I go over there to pray." He took Peter and Zebedee's two sons, James and John, and he became anguished and distressed. He told them, "My soul is crushed with grief to the point of death. Stay here and keep watch with me."

He went on a little farther and bowed with his face to the ground, praying, "My Father! If it is possible, let this cup of suffering be taken away from me. Yet I want your will to be done, not mine."

Then he returned to the disciples and found them asleep. He said to Peter, "Couldn't you watch with me even one hour? Keep watch and pray, so that you will not give in to temptation. For the spirit is willing, but the body is weak!"

Then Jesus left them a second time and prayed, "My Father! If this cup cannot be taken away unless I drink it, your will be done." When he returned to them again, he found them sleeping, for they couldn't keep their eyes open.

So he went to pray a third time, saying the same things again. — Matthew 26:36–44 (NLT)

What would you pray if your life were in mortal danger? If you knew you would soon face intense suffering, what would you ask God for?

Most of us would want to be rescued. We would beg God to get us out of there fast, whatever it took. Jesus didn't want to suffer, either. When He prayed in the garden, He was in anguish over what was about to happen. He asked God to spare Him, but that wasn't the end of His prayer. That wasn't the final word. He said, *"Yet I want your will to be done, not mine"* (Matthew 26:39 NLT). He was saying, "Father, You know best, so if this is the way You say it should be, so be it."

This isn't the only instance where we read of Jesus praying for God's will to be done. In the sample prayer Jesus gave His disciples, which we know as the Lord's Prayer, Jesus said, *"Thy kingdom come, Thy will be done in earth, as it is in heaven"* (Matthew 6:10 KJV). *Thy will be done.*

Our prayer lives tend to be based on "my will be done" instead of "Thy will be done." We make our requests of God, and if things don't turn out the way we think they should, we accuse God of not answering our prayers. We start to doubt that He hears them, that He cares, or that He even exists. If we don't think God is answering our prayers, we need to stop and consider what we mean by answers.

We read in 1 John 5:14–15, *"And we are confident that he hears us whenever we ask for anything that pleases him. And since we know he hears us when we make our requests, we also know that he will give us what we ask for"* (NLT). There's an 'if' to getting what we ask from God: our requests need to please Him. When we're struggling to receive answers to our prayers, it's probably because we're missing the "Thy will be done."

Finding God's Will

God's Will and Scripture

Okay, so if we should be praying for God's will, how in the world are we supposed to know what that is? Do we float around aimlessly in the dark, hoping God's hand will push us here and there? No, God didn't leave us in the dark. If we're truly interested in knowing God's will, we need look no further than the Bible. God gave us a whole book full of information about who He is and what He wants. Scripture is knowledge of God revealed to us by Him.

Take, for instance, Micah 6:8: *"He hath shewed thee, O man, what is good; and what doth the LORD require of thee, but to do justly, and to love mercy, and to walk humbly with thy God?"* (KJV). We could base our entire lives on this verse, but there is plenty more where that came from. The Bible contains guidelines for how God wants us to think, speak, and act and covers the full range of human experience and relationships.

Second Timothy 3:16 reads, *"All Scripture is inspired by God and is useful to teach us what is true and to make us realize what is wrong in our lives. It corrects us when we are wrong and teaches us to do what is right"* (NLT). If we want answers about God's will regarding how we should live and what decisions we should make, all we have to do is read the Bible and keep reading it.

God's Will and the Holy Spirit

God not only gave us His Word, He also placed inside all believers a part of Him, His own Spirit, to guide us in His will. Jesus told His disciples, *"I am telling you these things now while I am still with you. But when the Father sends the Advocate as my representative—that is, the Holy Spirit—he will teach you everything and will remind you of everything I have told you"* (John 14:25–26 NLT).

The Holy Spirit also performs the special function of praying for us in a way that is pleasing to God:

> *And the Holy Spirit helps us in our weakness. For example, we don't know what God wants us to pray for. But the Holy Spirit prays for us with groanings that cannot be expressed in words. And the Father who knows all hearts knows what the Spirit is saying, for the Spirit pleads for us believers in harmony with God's own will.* — **Romans 8:26–27 (NLT)**

God gives us everything we need to discern His will. We say, "I don't know what to do. I need to hear the voice of God." If we are reading Scripture daily and paying attention to the promptings of the Holy Spirit within us, it isn't hard to hear God's voice. What we sometimes want is for God to tell us something different.

"Hallowed Be Thy Name"

The first line of the Lord's Prayer points to an important aspect of God's will that we may be missing or misunderstanding: *"Our Father which art in heaven, Hallowed be thy name"* (Matthew 6:9 KJV). The New Living Translation reads, *"Our Father in heaven, may your name be kept holy"* (Matthew 6:9 NLT).

We often get confused in our prayer life and ask God for things that will glorify us. God isn't out to glorify us. He is concerned with His own glory.

We read in Ezekiel:

Then I was concerned for my holy name, on which my people brought shame among the nations.

Therefore, give the people of Israel this message from the Sovereign LORD: I am bringing you back, but not because you deserve it. I am doing it to protect my holy name, on which you brought shame while you were scattered among the nations. I will show how holy my great name is—the name on which you brought shame among the nations. And when I reveal my holiness through you before their very eyes, says the Sovereign LORD, then the nations will know that I am the LORD. For I will gather you up from all the nations and bring you home again to your land. — Ezekiel 36:21–24 (NLT)

God's people were in captivity. They had been taken from their homeland. They were in bondage. They had lost their land, their livelihoods, their family members, and their place of worship. They were outcasts. They were ashamed, and God said their shame reflected badly on Him. Other nations were mocking God's name because of the poor circumstances of His people (Ezekiel 36:20). They thought God's people were suffering because God was unable to protect and help them though actually they were being punished (Ezekiel 36:17–20).

God decided to restore His people and return them to their homeland, not because they no longer deserved punishment and should be let off the hook for good behavior but because God wanted everyone to know the truth of who He is. He is the Holy God, the Sovereign God, all-powerful and able to save.

When God answers our prayers, when He delivers us from trouble, helps us to overcome obstacles, and provides for us, it's not because we in any way deserve it. He does these things to protect and glorify His holy name. He wants people to know His true character—who He really is.

Let's stop trying to make our own names great and seek to glorify God instead. This starts with being honest with ourselves, with God, and with others about how undeserving we are. If we believe that we have earned what God gives us or are entitled to it, we will not give Him the glory He is due. When the blessing comes, we give the impression that we're blessed because of what we did. We were good. We prayed. We made the right decisions. Our self-righteousness rather than the goodness, grace, and power of God becomes the star of the story.

We need to be honest about the fact that we don't have it all together and can't do it all ourselves. Our weakness and deficiency serve a purpose: *"We now have this light shining in our hearts, but we ourselves are like fragile clay jars containing this great treasure. This makes it clear that our great power is from God, not from ourselves"* (2 Corinthians 4:7 NLT). When people look at our lives, they shouldn't see how great we are; they should see God at work.

I was in Miami recently and passed by 95th Street. For most people, 95th Street is nothing. But for me, 95th Street is a big deal. I got shot there—three shots to the back.

As we drove past 95th Street, I thought to myself, "That's the place where God decided that I was not going to die." He sent mercy out to break my fall. I couldn't save myself. I needed God's grace.

That's true of all of us spiritually. We don't deserve credit for being Christians. The reason we are saved is not because we found the Lord; it's because He found us. Jesus said, *"You didn't choose me. I chose you"* (John 15:16 NLT). Why did He choose us? Why did He make us His? He chose us so He would be glorified in us (John 17:10).

God has positioned us so that whenever He wants to draw attention to His Name on earth (to benefit others), He does something for us, in us, or through us. Maybe it's something we prayed for specifically, or maybe it's something we didn't realize we truly needed.

This doesn't mean God causes terrible things to happen just so He can get the glory. The world is full of sin and its far-reaching consequences. God is not responsible for that. God is perfect and holy. We read in James 1:13, *"God is never tempted to do wrong, and he never tempts anyone else"* (NLT). He is the giver of *"good and perfect"* gifts (James 1:17 NLT). The world is in desperate need of the untainted goodness only God can give, and He wants people to know it.

Our prayer lives must be adjusted to prioritize and seek God's glory. We should be praying, "Father, display the greatness of Your name by shining a light on what You are doing for me. Bring me out of my situation or strengthen me in it, according to Your will. I don't deserve it, Lord, and if You do this, people are going to know that I couldn't be doing it on my own. They will see Your work in my life."

Our prayers shouldn't be about how we are going to handle our problems or fix the situation. It's not about what we can do; it's about what God has done and will do. God is the One who gives us mercy, grace, strength, deliverance, wisdom, and material resources for all circumstances. He is the One who extends His hand to us. He is the One who blesses us with His love. We don't need to try harder and do better so we can earn God's favor and deserve His help before we come to Him. Our failures don't mean God can't use us. He knows what He is dealing with, and our weakness showcases the fullness of His power and the marvelous miracle of His grace.

If we are going to become vehicles for the revelation of God's holy name on the earth, we can't keep it a secret what God has done and is doing in our lives. Even as we are using the gifts, knowledge, resources, and opportunities God gives us, we can't make the victories about us. We can't take credit, or we are robbing God of the glory due His name.

It's important that people know we are Christians, not so they will think we are pure and righteous in ourselves but so that when God blesses us and answers our prayers, others will know it is because we belong to Christ. It is our purpose, our great privilege and responsibility, to be a testimony to the power, goodness, and love of God so others will know His name and His reputation on earth will match the truth of who He is.

Love

There is another fundamental aspect of God's will that should be reflected in our prayers: love. When Jesus was asked what the most important commandment was, He replied:

> *"You must love the LORD your God with all your heart, all your soul, and all your mind." This is the first and greatest commandment. A second is equally important: "Love your neighbor as yourself." The entire law and all the demands of the prophets are based on these two commandments. — **Matthew 22:37–40 (NLT)***

We shouldn't be tempted to dismiss these commandments as an Old Covenant matter, part of the law Christians no longer live under. Jesus told His disciples, *"So now I am giving you a new commandment: Love each other. Just as I have loved you, you should love each other"* (John 13:34 NLT). He said it again: *"This is my commandment: Love each other in the same way I have loved you. ... This is my command: Love each other"* (John 15:12, 17 NLT). Jesus even said, *"Love your enemies, bless them that curse you, do good to them that hate you, and pray for them which despitefully use you, and persecute you"* (Matthew 5:44 KJV).

Are our prayers loving? Are we honoring God, worshipping Him, and thanking Him? Do we consider the needs of others?

Philippians 2:3–4 reads, *"Don't be selfish; don't try to impress others. Be humble, thinking of others as better than yourselves. Don't look out only for your own interests, but take an interest in others, too"* (NLT). Too often when we pray, we're focused on what we want and what would benefit us. We are thinking of elevating ourselves, stepping on other people on our way to the top, and getting back at those who offend, mistreat, or overlook us.

This is not God's will. His commandment is love. He desires for us to have generous and compassionate hearts guided by the bountiful love He so graciously extends to us. Our prayers should always come from a place of love.

Grace to Love and Obey

Jesus said loving God is the most important thing for us to do, but what does it mean to love God?

Jesus told His disciples, *"All who love me will do what I say. My Father will love them, and we will come and make our home with each of them. Anyone who doesn't love me will not obey me"* (John 14:23–24 NLT).

Jesus also said, *"I have loved you even as the Father has loved me. Remain in my love. When you obey my commandments, you remain in my love, just as I obey my Father's commandments and remain in his love. ... You are my friends if you do what I command"* (John 15:9–10, 14 NLT).

Therefore, love and obedience are connected—which we don't necessarily want to hear. It would be so much easier if we could be free to live however we want and still receive the abundance of God's gifts! Oftentimes, our tendency is to want God to grant our every wish and get us out of trouble, whether we're trying to obey Him or not.

However, Scripture warns us against this way of thinking:

> *Don't be misled—you cannot mock the justice of God. You will always harvest what you plant. Those who live only to satisfy their own sinful nature will harvest decay and death from that sinful nature. But those who live to please the Spirit will harvest everlasting life from the Spirit.* — **Galatians 6:7–8 (NLT)**

God knows whether or not we're serious about having a relationship with Him on His terms. We read in 1 John:

> *And we can be sure that we know him if we obey his commandments. If someone claims, "I know God," but doesn't obey God's commandments, that person is a liar and is not living in the truth. But those who obey God's word truly show how completely they love him. That is how we know we are living in him. Those who say they*

live in God should live their lives as Jesus did. — *1 John 2:3–6 (NLT)*

Yet how can we possibly be obedient all of the time? We can't—not on our own! In and of ourselves, we don't have the capacity to love God in obedience, as the Old Covenant demanded and as Jesus, too, tells us we ought to love Him.

But here's the good news: Under the law, God made demands that we couldn't meet. Under the New Covenant, however, God meets His own demands through us, by way of His grace. Then we are able and empowered to do what He requires of us! As we read in Paul's letter to the Philippians:

I can do everything through Christ, who gives me strength. — *Philippians 4:13 (NLT)*

Through grace, then, we even have the strength to love God and others freely and completely.

If we are willfully living outside of the moral guidelines God gives us in the Bible, then we shouldn't expect to get the answers we want when we pray. But if we lean on God's goodness, not our own, in our prayers and in our daily life, His grace will empower us to obey Him and love each other.

Faith

Choosing to follow God's Word even when it goes against what we feel or what other people tell us is right requires faith—faith in God's sovereignty, faith in the perfection of His will, and faith in the truth of Scripture. This faith is essential to effective prayer:

> *Then Jesus said to the disciples, "Have faith in God. I tell you the truth, you can say to this mountain, 'May you be lifted up and thrown into the sea,' and it will happen. But you must really believe it will happen and have no doubt in your heart. I tell you, you can pray for anything, and if you believe that you've received it, it will be yours." — Mark 11:22–24 (NLT)*

If we want answers to our prayers, we must believe that God is going to give us what He says He will—not anything in the world but anything in the Word. We have to receive the finished work before we see the final result. Prayer is not just a wish, a thought, or a hope; it's one of the most basic acts of faith.

Living by Faith Means Living Prayerfully

Believing in who God is, in what He says He has done and will do, in His power and infallibility, and in His love for us moves us to an understanding of how much we need Him. Prayer is an expression of our dependence on God.

Praying from faith means we don't see prayer as a backup plan, a last resort, or a roll of the dice. We don't shrug our shoulders and say, "Prayer couldn't hurt." We know with absolute certainty that prayer will help. There is no way that *prayerfulness* and *prayerlessness* could produce the same results.

Living prayerfully means we start with prayer. We base our entire lives on our connection with God. There is no area of our lives that we leave out of our prayers. We don't get too busy to pray because we understand that the more we are doing, the more we need to pray.

Any area of our lives that is failing reveals our failure to pray. It is a defining characteristic of human nature to believe that we can handle things on our own. If we think we don't need God, He may allow us to experience situations that reveal how much we really do need Him. When we are overwhelmed or backed into a corner, we cry out to God, "I can't do this alone!" We realize our need.

The key is not to wait until things go south and then try to play catch-up with our prayer life. Living prayerfully means maintaining that faith-driven, humbly dependent connection with God at all times.

Prayer is a way of life, and every church should have a prayer culture. We need to view prayer as a problem solver in our churches. We need to agree that preaching is not enough to bring saints to maturity in the Lord and we can't grow spiritually if we don't pray. We must understand that the morality of our churches depends upon our commitment to trusting God as the Lord of the house. Everything in the church needs prayer as the impetus and engine behind it, and we can't maintain a functioning church without praying together.

While corporate prayer is essential to healthy and productive churches, it cannot take the place of private prayer. After fifteen years of going to corporate prayer, I reached the point where I realized I needed to make other arrangements if I was going to talk to God quietly. People started looking for counseling sessions at corporate prayer. I would be down on my knees, praying, and someone would come up and tap me on the shoulder, asking, "Can I talk to you for a minute?"

It's critical for us to remember that God wants a personal relationship with each of us, which means we spend time talking with Him about ourselves. Sometimes we try to outsource our prayer life, asking other people to pray for us but neglecting to pray on our own. On the flip side of the coin, we can become so concerned about praying for our churches, our country, and our world and trying to pray other people into the presence of God that we don't pray for ourselves.

We can't afford to be so busy praying about other people's problems that we forget to spend time looking into our own souls and seeing our personal need for God. Let's not be so anxious to confess other people's sin that we fail to face our own. We need to spend time every day in intense but organic fellowship with God, talking with Him about our own lives.

If we commit to living from a place of real, prayerful faith that results in full dependence on God—His truth, His will, His might, His love, and His grace—then we can fully expect the power of God to be revealed in our lives and our churches in awesome ways.

Making Way for God's Will

Dependence on God requires us to get out of our own way. We tend to get caught up in our own understanding of a situation. When we pray, we present God with a to-do list: "All right, God, this is what needs to happen." We expect Him to make everything come together in the way we see it playing out for the best, and if He doesn't deliver, we start questioning His ability and intentions. We think maybe He didn't hear us or He doesn't care. We wonder why He didn't change this circumstance or keep that obstacle from becoming a problem. What we are forgetting is that we don't know everything.

It is the human way to struggle for control. We don't just want to be on top of the situation; we try to get over it, around it, and all up in it. Let's make it our business to get over ourselves and move out of the way so God can do His work. We don't always know how best to handle things because our perspective is limited. Our view of the situation is incomplete. We can't see the big picture and all of the pieces that contribute to it; only God can.

God said to Jeremiah, *"Call unto me, and I will answer thee, and show thee great and mighty things, which thou knowest not"* (Jeremiah 33:3 KJV). These "great and mighty things" are the things beyond us. The word 'great' in the Hebrew language is a word that points to *important* things that are critical to solving complicated and seemingly insurmountable problem.

Sometimes our prayers are inaccurate because we target the minor, offshoot issues of a situation and not the major issue. This leaves us praying random prayers. When God reveals the important things to us, we can pray specifically and get better results.

The word 'mighty' also carries great significance in the original Hebrew language. It speaks of unsearchable or "inaccessible" things,[3] which we could never figure out on our own without God's help. Because of their "fenced in" nature,[4] mighty things are only discovered as they are revealed by God through prayer.

Instead of directing God to do this or that to make everything turn out as we think it should, we should take a time-out and pray for wisdom: "What is really going on here, God? What can I do to make way for Your will?" When we pray, we're often looking for a change in circumstances, but sometimes what we truly need is a change in perspective.

In Numbers 13 and 14, we read of an instance where the Israelites had a perspective problem. When some leaders of the Israelites went to explore the land God had promised to give them, they came back with news of the goodness of the land but also the strength of the current residents. They had even seen giants. Most of the men who had explored the land were afraid. They were intimidated at the thought of having to conquer the peoples who already lived there, so they spread a bad report about how impossible they would be to defeat. The Israelites turned against God and refused to take the land as He intended. As a result, God sent them back into the desert until all of that generation had died—except for the two men who trusted Him.

The people believed they were not able to take the land even though God had promised to give it to them. They were thinking in terms of their own apparent inability to handle the obstacles they saw before them. They trusted their own understanding of the situation instead of having faith in God's ability to make a way for them.

Do we trust God enough to take what He gives us, or do we let our own perceptions and emotions get in the way of what God wants to do in and through us to help others and advance His kingdom? Unless we choose to put faith in God over everyone and everything else, we will never step into the full blessings He has already prepared for us. We will shrink back in fear, stall out in discouragement, or take a detour that removes us from the mission God designed us to fulfill.

The scope and intricacy of God's work are beyond us. He weaves together more details in the physical and spiritual realms than we can begin to comprehend, and He knows all things from before the beginning of time through all eternity.

It's better to go with God's plan, even if we can't see how all of the parts are coming together. What looks to us like a curveball or an insurmountable obstacle is no surprise to God. He knew all along, and He has it covered.

If we understood it all fully, if we could see all things, if we could do it all ourselves, we wouldn't need faith and we wouldn't need God. We read in Proverbs, *"Trust in the* LORD *with all your heart; do not depend on your own understanding. Seek his will in all you do, and he will show you which path to take"* (Proverbs 3:5–6 NLT).

Only God can reliably show us the right way every time, and He doesn't keep it to Himself. He will make sure we know what to do if we truly trust Him and submit to His direction. When we pray, we must choose to trust God's perspective over ours. We also need to rest in the teachings of Jesus and in God's promises as revealed in Scripture. When we rest in God's will, we leave room for His work.

CONCLUSION

Resting in the Lord

Following Jesus and depending on God lead the believer into a place of rest:

> *Then Jesus said, "Come to me, all of you who are weary and carry heavy burdens, and I will give you rest. Take my yoke upon you. Let me teach you, because I am humble and gentle at heart, and you will find rest for your souls. For my yoke is easy to bear, and the burden I give you is light."* — **Matthew 11:28–30 (NLT)**

The promise of a light and easy burden and the concept of resting in God's will can be offensive to American sensibilities in particular because of this culture's mentality of striving and self-reliance and its worship of the human intellect. We believe that if we think hard enough, we'll figure it out, and if we work hard enough, we'll get it done—and woe to anyone who gets in our way!

Isn't leaning on God just a crutch? Isn't waiting on God just an excuse not to do anything for ourselves? How can we expect success if we sit around on our lazy butts, whining to God about our problems?

From a worldly perspective, faith may seem like an easy way out. Even Christians will say, "God helps those who help themselves." That's another misguided cliché. We think we need to work hard and get to a certain place in our lives to earn God's favor if we want to receive His love and blessings, but that's not the truth revealed to us in Scripture.

We shouldn't wait until we have it all figured out and under control before we turn to God and speak with Him about what's on our minds. We need His help, and He wants us to have it. If we wait until we're good enough, we will never have a relationship with God. He has already made provision in the finished work of Christ so we can approach Him in our imperfection, and He has already made provision for whatever it is we are praying about.

Relying on God doesn't mean doing nothing; it means doing what God tells us to do. Resting in the Lord means letting go of what we think we know and saying, "Thy will be done." God wants us to lay down our mental struggle and take Him at His word. If God says something is true—whether regarding moral conduct, our standing before Him, or His nature and purposes— we need to accept it and live from it regardless of what we see, hear, or feel that would seem to contradict it.

If we do this, God will give us a gift of immeasurable value to bless our lives in this turbulent and troubled world:

> *Be anxious for nothing, but in everything by prayer and supplication, with thanksgiving, let your requests be made known to God; and the peace of God, which surpasses all understanding, will guard your hearts and minds through Christ Jesus.* — **Philippians 4:6–7 (NKJV)**

We surrender our concerns to God in prayer, and He gives us peace. Whatever other answer He gives us, we can be at peace. Jesus said, *"I am leaving you with a gift—peace of mind and heart. And the peace I give is a gift the world cannot give. So don't be troubled or afraid"* (John 14:27 NLT).

This isn't the peace of mind that comes from job security, a full fridge, and a clean bill of health. It's a peace that holds you together when you go home with a pink slip instead of a paycheck. It's a peace that helps you change course when you and your spouse's five-year plan is shot to pieces by the unexpected. It's a peace that can steady you when you lose someone you love, when you get cancer in your thirties, when you don't know where your next meal is coming from. It's a peace that surpasses understanding. It's beyond anything that comes from or belongs to this world because it isn't of this world. It's a gift from God's own Spirit.

Notes

1. Zodhiates, Spiros, ed. *The Complete Word Study Dictionary: New Testament*. Word Study Series. AMG Publishers, 1992.
2. "Matthew 18:19." *Bible Hub*. http://biblehub.com/lexicon/matthew/18-19.htm
3. "Jeremiah 33:3." *Pulpit Commentary*. In *Bible Hub*. http://biblehub.com/commentaries/jeremiah/33-3.htm
4. "Jeremiah 33:3." *Cambridge Bible for Schools and Colleges*. In *Bible Hub*. http://biblehub.com/commentaries/jeremiah/33-3.htm

About the Author

Hart Ramsey, Sr., is the founder and Senior Pastor of Northview Christian Church in Dothan / Montgomery, Alabama, and Atlanta, Georgia. Pastor Ramsey is heralded for his relevant teaching of Kingdom truths through the anointing of Jesus Christ. His goal is to offer simple insight into difficult issues with a straightforward, passionate approach to life and ministry. He is the founder of Hart Ramsey Media, LLC, and the nationally acclaimed daily text ministry "Hart Ramsey's UPLIFT," which provides inspiration and hope to thousands across the country. Pastor Ramsey is an accomplished author and musician, a published song writer, and a certified recording engineer.

About Sermon To Book

SermonToBook.com began with a simple belief: that sermons should be touching lives, *not* collecting dust. That's why we turn sermons into high-quality books that are accessible to people all over the globe.

Turning your sermon series into a book exposes more people to God's Word, better equips you for counseling, accelerates future sermon prep, adds credibility to your ministry, and even helps make ends meet during tight times.

John 21:25 tells us that the world itself couldn't contain the books that would be written about the work of Jesus Christ. Our mission is to try anyway. Because, in heaven, there will no longer be a need for sermons or books. Our time is now.

If God so leads you, we'd love to work with you on your sermon or sermon series.

Visit www.sermontobook.com to learn more.

Made in the USA
Monee, IL
01 November 2019

16207611R00033